miniature schnauzer

understanding and caring for your breed

D1331594

Written by
Jeanette Wilson

miniature schnauzer

understanding and
caring for your breed

Written by
Jeanette Wilson

Pet Book Publishing Company

The Old Hen House, St Martin's Farm, Zeals, Warminster, Wiltshire, BA12 6NZ.

Printed and bound in South Korea through Pacom.

All rights reserved. No part of this work may be reproduced, in any form or by any means, electronic or mechanical, including photocopying, recording or by any information storage and retrieval system, without the prior written permission of the publisher.

Copyright © Pet Book Publishing Company 2015.

Every reasonable care has been taken in the compilation of this publication. The Publisher and Author cannot accept liability for any loss, damage, injury or death resulting from the keeping of Miniature Schnauzers by user(s) of this publication, or from the use of any materials, equipment, methods or information recommended in this publication or from any errors or omissions that may be found in the text of this publication or that may occur at a future date, except as expressly provided by law.

The 'he' pronoun is used throughout this book instead of the rather impersonal 'it', however no gender bias is intended.

ISBN: 978-1-906305-75-8
ISBN: 1-906305-75-7

Acknowledgements

The publishers would like to thank the following for help with photography: Judy Childerley (Chidegait), Kirsty Sanders (Zakmayo), Katherine Browning and Scruffy.

Contents

Introducing the Miniature Schnauzer

Smart, lively, and playful, the Miniature Schnauzer is a superb companion dog. Looking out from under his bushy eyebrows, he is always on the alert, keen to take part in whatever is going on. He also has a gentle side to his nature, and will give you boundless love and affection.

The Miniature Schnauzer was bred down from the larger Standard Schnauzer, a dog valued as a formidable ratter and a fearless watchdog. The Mini Schnauzer's primary role was to be a companion dog, but he retains many of the characteristics of his ancestors.

Physical characteristics

There can be few breeds that are more conveniently-sized than the Miniature Schnauzer. He measures 30 to 35cm (12 to 14 inches) at the shoulder, which makes him a substantial little dog – bigger and more robust than the Toy breeds, but small enough to adapt to any size of home.

The overwhelming impression is one of smartness; the Mini Schnauzer has a neat, square-shaped body, which is complemented by a brick-shaped head. He moves with a forward-reaching, purposeful gait, which sums up his outgoing personality.

The coat is harsh and wiry, but it is the 'furnishings' – the longer hair – that makes the Mini Schnauzer. In contrast to the tight-fitting coat on his body, he has longer hair on the legs, underside and hindquarters. The longer hair on his head forms remarkable busy eyebrows, and a distinguished-looking moustache and beard. When a Miniature Schnauzer is presented in the show ring, with his coat trimmed to perfection, he is, indeed, an impressive sight.

The Miniature Schnauzer comes in variety of colors.

- Pepper and salt: This is the most common of the available colors, and it is unique to Schnauzers. The guard hairs on the top coat are banded to give a mosaic of black/grey coloring. The furnishings are lighter in color. Puppies are born with a dark coat, and this lightens as they mature. There is considerable variation in shades of pepper and salt in adult Miniature Schnauzers.

- Black: A striking pure black.

- Black and Silver: The black body coat contrasts with silver markings.

- White: Not seen in the USA, but this color is now recognized in most other countries.

The black Miniature Schnauzer is highly distinctive.

Allergy sufferers

The Miniature Schnauzer's coat does not shed in the same way as most other breeds, therefore he is potentially a good choice for those that suffer with allergies.

However, there is a minimal amount of shedding, and sometimes allergies are caused by dandruff or saliva, so there are no guarantees for allergy sufferers.

The best plan is to spend some time with Miniature Schnauzers and monitor reactions before making a commitment to buy a puppy.

Temperament

What can you expect if you bring a Miniature Schnauzer into your home? There is one thing you can be certain of – life will never be quite the same...

The Mini Schnauzer is a relatively small dog, but he has a huge personality. He finds the world a fascinating place and wants to investigate everything, and everybody, that comes his way. He is one of the most companionable of breeds; he simply wants to be where his people are. He must learn to cope with time on his own, but he will be utterly miserable if he is excluded for lengthy periods.

The Mini Schnauzer has an exemplary temperament which make him an ideal therapy dog.

Beware of the watchdog in your midst! The Mini Schnauzer takes his guarding duties very seriously and will be ever ready to warn you of the approach of strangers. This is an asset so long as you do not allow it to get out of hand. A warning bark is desirable; a dog who will not be quiet, or one that runs up and down the garden fence, barking continuously, is not. This all comes down to training and leadership, which are important factors when taking on a Miniature Schnauzer.

Family dog

Children and Miniature Schnauzers go well together, but you must ensure that a sense of mutual respect is established from the word go. Children must learn not to tease or to play games that provoke over-excitement. They must also understand that there are times when a dog should not be disturbed, particularly when he is eating or when he is sleeping.

On the other side of the coin, a Miniature Schnauzer must learn to respect all members of his human pack, no matter how small they are. Interactions should be closely supervised, so that he learns that jumping up, mouthing or nipping is not acceptable behaviour. If you get relations off to a good start, you will be rewarded with a wonderful companion who is loving and affectionate with all members of his family.

Life expectancy

We are fortunate that the Miniature Schnauzer is a healthy breed with a good life expectancy. Most will reach their early teens, and some may do even better.

Tracing back in time

The Miniature Schnauzer has a relatively recent history, but it is interesting to trace back how and why the Schnauzer breeds were developed.

There are three varieties of Schnauzer:

Giant Schnauzer: A large dog, measuring 23 to 27 inches (58 to 68cm) at the shoulder.

Standard Schnauzer: A medium-sized dog measuring 17 to 20 inches (42 to 50cm).

Miniature Schnauzer: The smallest variety, measuring 12 to14 inches (30 to 35cm).

Standard Schnauzer

This is the original member of the Schnauzer family. A type of dog very similar to the Standard Schnauzer was popular in the 14 or 15th century in southern Germany, where he was used as an all-purpose farm

Facing page: The Giant Schnauzer.

dog. He was employed as a drover, moving livestock from place to place. He was a formidable ratter in the stables, and was a useful watchdog, warning of the approach of strangers. This versatile dog would also pull a cart to market if required.

In the 19th century, German breeders added new breeds to the mix, such as the black German Poodle and the Wirehaired Pinscher, to create the breed we now know as the Standard Schnauzer.

Giant Schnauzer

The giant variety was developed in the early 20th century when the Germans were experimenting with the most suitable breeds to use as police dogs. Breeders crossed black Great Danes with the Standard Schnauzer with the aim of producing a large, impressive dog with strong protective instincts. His role was as a deterrent, barking a warning rather than being overtly aggressive.

Miniature Schnauzer

The smallest member of the Schnauzer family was developed to be a smaller, more compact version of the Standard Schnauzer, and was particularly sought after as a ratter in the home and farm, as well as being an alert watchdog.

In many instances, down-sizing a breed entails selecting the smallest representatives for breeding.

But this was not the case with the Miniature Schnauzer. In the late 19th century, good examples of Standards were crossed with smaller breeds, such as the Affenpinscher and the Pomeranian, as well as the rough-coated German Terrier and the Poodle, to achieve the perfect Schnauzer in miniature.

Naming the breed

Where does the name Schnauzer come from? Interestingly, it is the only breed that takes its name from one of its own kind.

In a dog show in Hanover in 1879, the winner of the rough-haired Pinscher class was a dog called Schnauzer, which means 'beard' or 'snout'. In the early days, Schnauzers were also referred to as German Rough-haired Terriers.

The Standard Schnauzer: The Miniature Schnauzer is a down-sized version of this breed.

Developing the breed

The first Miniature Schnauzer was exhibited as a breed in its own right in 1899. Since that time, interest in the smallest Schnauzer has escalated, and in terms of popularity, he now outstrips both the Standard and the Giant. In both the USA and the UK, the Miniature Schnauzer is listed in the top 15 most popular breeds.

Going global

Right from the beginning there have been strong links between Germany and the USA in the development of the Miniature Schnauzer. The breed reached American shores in 1924, and was recognized by the American Kennel Club in 1926.

The new breed was included in the Terrier Group because of his ratting ancestry, which he shares with many of the terrier breeds. However, he was not bred to 'go to ground' like so many of the British terriers, and is more correctly termed a Pinscher – a 'biter'.

The AKC retains the Miniature Schnauzer in its Terrier Group to this day, although it is classified in the Utility Group in the UK and it is included in a section for Schnauzers and Pinschers in most other countries.

Miniature Schnauzers first came to the UK in 1928 and were known as Affenschnauzers. To begin with they were registered with Standard Schnauzers, but they were recognized as a distinct breed in 1932.

Throughout the development of the breed in the 20th and 21st centuries, the USA has proved to be highly influential, and many outstanding dogs have been produced. American-bred dogs have been exported and they have formed the bedrock of breeding programs in the UK, and in many other countries worldwide.

What should a Mini Schnauzer look like?

The Miniature Schnauzer, so smart and full of character, draws admiring glances wherever he goes. In the show ring, when he is groomed to perfection, he stands out a mile. So what makes a Mini Schnauzer so special?

The aim of breeders is to produce dogs that are sound, healthy, typical examples of their chosen breed, in terms of both looks and temperament To achieve this, they are guided by a Breed Standard, which is a written blueprint describing what the perfect specimen should look like.

Of course, there is no such thing as a 'perfect' dog, but breeders aspire to produce dogs that conform as closely as possible to the picture in words presented

by the Breed Standard. In the show ring, judges use the Breed Standard to assess the dogs before them, and it is the dog that, in their opinion, comes closest to the ideal, that will win top honours.

This has significance beyond the sport of showing, for the dogs that win in the ring will be used for breeding. The winners of today are therefore responsible for passing on their genes to future generations and preserving the breed in its best form.

There are some differences in Breed Standards depending on national kennel clubs. The American Standard is more descriptive than the English version. The Federation Cynologique International, which is the governing body for 86 countries, including Germany – the breed's homeland, also provides a highly-detailed and informative Standard.

General appearance

Small, stocky and robust in build, the Miniature Schnauzer is well balanced and appears smart and stylish. In terms of shape, the Mini Schnauzer is square – his body length is equal to his height at the shoulders – and he is characterized by a keen, alert expression. The UK Standard notes that correct conformation is of more importance than color, or any other 'beauty' points.

Temperament

The defining term for the Miniature Schnauzer is "alert". The Standards stress that he is primarily a companion dog, willing to please and obedient to command. He is also described as "reliable", which sums up his genuine nature.

Head and skull

The Miniature Schnauzer is known as a 'head breed', meaning that this is his outstanding feature. The head is strong and of good length; its width diminishes slightly from ears to eyes and, again, to the tip of the nose. The stop, which is the indentation between the muzzle and the forehead, is moderate, to accentuate the prominent eyebrows. The muzzle is powerful, ending in a blunt line, with a bristly moustache and chin whiskers. The nose is black with wide nostrils.

Ears

In the UK, and countries governed by the FCI, cropping is illegal, and the Miniature has natural V-shaped ears that are set on high and drop forwards towards the temple. Cropped ears, which are seen on American dogs, should be in balance with the head, and should not be exaggerated in length.

Eyes

The eyes are medium-sized, according to the UK and FCI Standards, but are described as "small" by the American Standard. However, all agree that they are set forward, enhanced by the bushy eyebrows. They are dark in color with a keen expression.

Mouth

The jaws are strong and the teeth meet in a scissor bite, with the teeth on the upper jaw closely overlapping the teeth on the lower jaw.

Neck

The neck is strong and "nobly arched", according to the FCI Standard. It blends smoothly into the shoulders; the skin on the throat is tight-fitting.

Facing page: In the USA, Mini Schnauzers may have cropped ears.

Forequarters

The forelegs are straight and parallel when viewed from all sides; the elbows are close to the body. The sloping shoulders are muscled, but the shoulder blade lies close against the ribcage. The pasterns, which act as the shock absorbers on the front legs, are short and springy.

Body

The chest is moderately broad, and the back is strong with a topline that slopes slightly from the withers (the highest point of the shoulders) to the base of the tail. The square shape is typical of the breed, and there should be no hint of coarseness or exaggeration.

Hindquarters

The hindquarters are strong and muscled; they are well bent at the stifle (the dog's 'knee'). The hocks (equivalent to our ankles) are strong, very well angulated, turning neither in nor out.

Feet

Short, round and cat-like with thick, black pads. The toes are arched and compact.

Tail

In the UK, and countries governed by the FCI, the tail is now left at its natural length. It is set on high, and is of moderate length, thick at the base and tapering towards the top. The tail should be carried jauntily. In the US, tails are still docked. The tail is set on high and carried erect, and should be of sufficient length to be clearly visible over the backline of the body.

Contrasting tails: full (left), docked (right).

Gait/movement

When the Miniature Schnauzer is trotting he should have good reach in the forequarters with the driving power coming from behind. The movement should appear free, balanced and vigorous.

Coat

The breed is double-coated with a dense undercoat and a harsh, wiry topcoat. The furnishings – the longer hair on the head and legs – should be fairly thick, but not silky.

Colour

The traditional colors for the Miniature Schnauzer are pepper and salt, black and silver, and black. Pure white Miniature Schnauzers are now recognized by the FCI and the Kennel Club in the UK, but this color is not accepted by the American Kennel Club.

Pepper and salt is a combination of black and white banded hairs and solid black and white unbanded hairs; the banded hairs should predominate. All shades are acceptable.

Black and silver is a striking color combination; dogs are solid black with silver markings on the eyebrows, muzzle, chest, legs, and under the tail.

Size

The UK Standard gives an ideal height of 14 inches (35cm) for dogs, and 13 inches (33cm) for females. The American Standard and the FCI Standard do not differentiate between the sexes, with dogs and bitches accepted at 12 to 14 inches (30 to 35cm),

Summing up

Although the majority of Mini Schnauzers are pet dogs and will never be exhibited in the show ring, it is important that breeders strive for perfection and try to produce dogs that adhere as closely as possible to the Breed Standard. This ensures that the Miniature Schnauzer remains sound in mind and body, and retains the unique characteristics of this very special breed.

What do you want from your Mini schnauzer?

There are hundreds of dog breeds to choose from, so how can you be sure that the Miniature Schnauzer is the right one for you? Before you take the plunge into Mini Schnauzer ownership, weigh up the pros and cons so you can be 100 per cent confident that this is the breed that is best suited to your lifestyle.

Companion

The Miniature Schnauzer has inherited working traits from his ancestors; he is an excellent ratter and watchdog, but it is in the role of companion that he excels. The Mini Schnauzer is a natural fit in a family, and he thrives on being part of a busy household.

However, his working history does continue to play a part in his make up. The Standard Schnauzer was valued for his adaptability and his ability to think for himself, and you will see these traits in the miniature version.

The Mini Schnauzer will fit in with all types of families and lifestyles; he is good with children and will be an enthusiastic playmate. He will equally suit older owners, with a more sedate lifestyle. He will be loving and affectionate with all members of the family, but you may find that he has a special favourite that he sticks closely to.

Although you want to encourage your Mini Schnauzer to bond closely with his human family, make sure you train him to cope with periods on his own. This is a breed that can become too people dependant, and, without proper training, he may become very anxious when he is left alone. This will take the form of constant barking, or destructive behavior, and so it is vital that this is nipped in the bud. From the time your puppy comes home, accustom him to spending short periods on his own – ideally when he is safe and secure in an indoor crate – and he will understand that although you go away, you always come back.

Watchdog

The Miniature Schnauzer is a great watchdog – and the sound he makes suggests a far bigger dog. This is a plus point if you want to be warned of the approach of visitors, but make sure you keep it under control. A Miniature Schnauzer will start barking – but he wont necessarily stop – unless you train him to be "Quiet", and then reward him for co-operating.

Show dog

Do you have ambitions to exhibit your Miniature Schnauzer in the show ring? This is a specialist sport, which often becomes highly addictive, but you must have the right dog to start with.

It takes a breed specialist to evaluate whether a puppy has show potential.

If you plan to show your Mini Schnauzer, you need to track down a show quality puppy, then train him so he will perform in the show ring, and accept the detailed 'hands on' examination that he will be subjected to when he is being judged.

You will also have to become an expert groomer, or employ the services of a professional. The Miniature Schnauzer is very high maintenance in terms of show presentation, so you will need to be truly dedicated to this highly-specialized art.

For more information, see page 60.

It is also important to bear in mind that not every puppy with show potential develops into a top-quality specimen, and so you must be prepared to love your Mini Schnauzer and give him a home for life, even if he doesn't make the grade.

Sports dog

If you are interested having a dog to compete in one of the canine sports, the intelligent Miniature Schnauzer will be more than willing. He likes to use his brains and will make his mark in competitive obedience, rally O and agility. For more information on dog sports, see page 152.

Facing page: The Mini Schnauzer is an able competitor in canine sports.

What does your Mini Schnauzer want from you?

A dog cannot speak for himself, so we need to view the world from a canine perspective and work out what a Miniature Schnauzer needs in order to live a happy, contented and fulfilling life.

Time and commitment

First of all, a Mini Schnauzer needs a commitment that you will care for him for the duration of his life – guiding him through his puppyhood, enjoying his adulthood, and being there for him in his later years. If all potential owners were prepared to make this pledge, there would be scarcely any dogs in rescue.

The Miniature Schnauzer was bred primarily to be a companion dog, and this is what he must be. If you cannot give your Mini Schnauzer the time and commitment he deserves, you would be strongly advised to delay owning a dog until your circumstances change.

Practical matters

The Miniature Schnauzer is an adaptable dog and will cope with varying amounts of exercise. He has the energy and endurance to enjoy long treks, but he is equally content with shorter outings, particularly if there is an element of variety. However, it is important to bear in mind that this is an active little dog and his exercise needs must not be neglected.

When it comes to coat care, you need to be very certain of what you are taking on. This is a high maintenance breed, and this applies to pet dogs as well as show dogs. A pet dog needs to be clipped on a regular basis, and show dogs must undergo the lengthy process of being hand-stripped, as well as being trimmed to enhance the unique Schnauzer look.

As a pet owner, you must budget for the services of a professional groomer in order to keep your Miniature Schnauzer clean and comfortable, as well making sure he looks his best.

Mental stimulation

The Miniature Schnauzer is quick to learn, but this is something of a double-edged sword as he will be equally quick to pick up both good and bad habits.

A well-trained Schnauzer is a joy to own, but you cannot leave this clever dog to his own devices. His philosophy is "give me an inch and I'll take a mile", and although he doesn't have an ounce of malice in his make up, a Mini Schnauzer allowed to rule the roost is no fun to live with. He will become very demanding – and if he doesn't get what he wants, he may bark at you until you give in.

As a responsible owner, you must give your dog a sense of leadership so he is happy to accept you as the decision-maker in the family. You must also give him the opportunity to use his brain. It does not matter what you do with him – training exercises, teaching tricks, trips out in the car, or going for new, interesting walks – all are equally appreciated, and will give your Miniature Schnauzer a purpose in life.

Extra considerations

Now you have decided that a Miniature Schnauzer is the dog for you, you can narrow your choice so you know exactly what you are looking for.

Male or female?

The decision as to whether you opt for a male or female really does come down to personal preference. In terms of size, there is little to choose between them; in the UK males are bred to be slightly larger, elsewhere both male and female are within the same height range.

A female Mini Schnauzer tends to look more feminine, so if you want a slightly more distinguished head, a male may be a better option, but most pet owners are more concerned about temperament. Both male and female Miniature Schnauzers are affectionate and fun-loving. Some owners reckon that females are better, but owners of males would swear the opposite! The

only certainty is that all dogs are individuals, and you can never second-guess how your dog is going to turn out.

You may find a female slightly more difficult to care for as you will need to cope with her seasonal cycle, which will start at around seven to eight months of age, with seasons occurring twice yearly thereafter. During the three-week period of a season, you will need to keep your female away from entire males (males that have not been neutered) to eliminate the risk of an unwanted pregnancy.

Many pet owners opt for neutering, which puts an end to the seasons, and also and has many attendant health benefits. The operation, known as spaying, is usually carried out at some point after the first season. The best plan is to seek advice from your vet.

An entire male may not cause many problems, although some do have a stronger tendency to mark, which could include in the house. However, training will usually put a stop to this. An entire male will also be on the lookout for females in season, and this may lead to difficulties, depending on your circumstances.

Neutering (castrating) a male is a relatively simple operation, and there are associated health benefits. Again, you should seek advice from your vet.

More than one?

Miniature Schnauzers are sociable dogs and certainly enjoy each other's company. But you would be wise to guard against the temptation of getting two puppies of similar ages, or two from the same litter.

Unfortunately there are some unscrupulous breeders who encourage people to do this, but they are thinking purely in terms of profit, and not considering the welfare of the puppies.

Looking after one puppy is hard work, but taking on two pups at the same time is more than double the workload. House training is a nightmare as, often, you don't even know which puppy is making mistakes, and training is impossible unless you separate the two puppies and give them one-on-one attention.

The puppies will never be bored as they have each other to play with. However, the likelihood is that the pair will form a close bond, and you will come a poor second.

If you do decide to add to your Mini Schnauzer population, wait at least 18 months so your first dog is fully trained and settled before taking on a puppy.

An older dog

You may decide to miss out on the puppy phase and take on an older dog instead. Such a dog may be harder to track down, but sometimes a breeder may have a youngster that is not suitable for showing, but is perfect for a family pet. In some cases, a breeder may re-home a female when her breeding career is at an end so she will enjoy the benefits of more individual attention.

There are advantages to taking on an older dog, as you know exactly what you are getting. But the upheaval of changing homes can be quite upsetting, so you will need to have plenty of patience during the settling in period.

Rehoming a rescued dog

We are fortunate that the number of Miniature Schnauzers that end up in rescue is relatively small, and this is often through no fault of the dog. The reasons are various, ranging from illness or death of the original owner to family breakdown, changing jobs, or even the arrival of a new baby.

It is unlikely that you will find a Mini Schnauzer in an all-breed rescue centre, but the specialist breed clubs run rescue schemes, and this will be your best option if you decide to go down this route.

Try to find out as much as you can about a dog's history so you know exactly what you are taking on. You need to be realistic about what you are capable of achieving so you can be sure you can give the dog in question a permanent home.

Again, you need to give a rescued Miniature Schnauzer plenty of time and patience as he settles into his new home, but if all goes well, you will have the reward of knowing that you have given your dog a second chance.

Sourcing
a puppy

Your aim is to find a healthy puppy that is typical of the breed, and has been reared with the greatest possible care. Where do you start?

A tried-and-trusted method of finding a puppy is to attend a dog show where your chosen breed is being exhibited. This will give you the opportunity to see lots of different Miniature Schnauzers, and although they may look the same at first glance, you will soon get your eye in and notice there are different 'types' on show. They are all pure-bred Mini Schnauzers, but breeders produce dogs with a family likeness, and so you can see which type you prefer.

When judging has been completed, talk to the exhibitors and find out more about their dogs. They may not have puppies available, but many will be planning a litter, and you may decide to put your name on a waiting list.

Internet research

The Internet is an excellent resource, but when it comes to finding a puppy, use it with care:

DO go to the website of your national Kennel Club.

Both the American Kennel Club (AKC) and the Kennel Club (KC) have excellent websites which will give you information about the Miniature Schnauzer as a breed, and what to look for when choosing a puppy. You will also find contact details for specialist breed clubs (see below).

Both sites have lists of puppies available, and you can look out for breeders of merit (AKC) and assured breeders (KC) which indicates that a code of conduct has been adhered to.

DO find details of specialist breed clubs.

On breed club websites you will find lots of useful information that will help you to care for your Mini Schnauzer. There may be contact details of breeders in your area, or you may need to go through the club secretary. Some websites also have a list of breeders that have puppies available. The advantage of going through a breed club is that members will follow a code of ethics, and this will give you some guarantees regarding breeding stock and health checks.

DO NOT look at puppies for sale.

There are legitimate Miniature Schnauzer breeders with their own websites, and they may, occasionally, advertise a litter, although in most cases reputable breeders have waiting lists for their puppies.

The danger comes from unscrupulous breeders who produce puppies purely for profit, with no thought for the health of the dogs they breed from and no care given to rearing the litter. Photos of puppies are hard to resist, but never make a decision based purely on an advertisement. You need to find out who the breeder is, and have the opportunity to visit their premises and inspect the litter before making a decision.

Questions, questions, questions

When you find a breeder with puppies available, you will have lots of questions to ask. These should include the following:

- Where have the puppies been reared? Hopefully, they will have been in a home environment which gives them the best possible start in life.

- How many are in the litter?

- What color are they?

- What is the split of males and females?

- How many have already been spoken for? The breeder will probably be keeping a puppy to show or for breeding, and there may be a number of potential purchasers on a waiting list.

Facing page: Take time to find a well-bred, healthy puppy.

- Can I see the mother with her puppies? The answer to this should always be 'yes'. Even if the breeder is in the process of weaning the puppies, you should still be given the opportunity to see mother and pups together.

- What age are the puppies?

- When will they be ready to go to their new homes?

Bear in mind puppies need to be with their mother and siblings until they are eight weeks of age otherwise they miss out on vital learning and communication skills which will have a detrimental effect on them for the rest of their lives.

You should also be prepared to answer a number of searching questions so the breeder can check if you are suitable as a potential owner of one of their precious puppies.

You will be asked some or all of the following:

- What is your home set up?

- Do you have children/grandchildren?

- What are their ages?

- Is there somebody at home most of the time?

- Have you considered the costs involved in coat care for this breed?

- What is your previous experience with dogs?

- Do you have plans to show your Miniature Schnauzer?

The breeder is not being intrusive; they need to understand the type of home you will be able to provide in order to make the right match. Do not be offended by this; the breeder is doing it for both the dog's benefit and also for yours.

Be very wary of a breeder who does not ask you questions. He or she may be more interested in making money out of the puppies rather than ensuring that they go to good homes. They may also have taken other short cuts which may prove disastrous in terms of veterinary bills or plain heartache.

Health issues

In common with all pure-bred dogs, the Miniature Schnauzer suffers from a few hereditary problems, and for the most part, these relate to eye conditions. In order to try to eliminate these from the breed, an annual eye examination can be carried out, and this should this should be considered essential for breeding stock.

For more information on inherited conditions, see page 184.

Puppy watching

Puppies are irresistible, and Miniature Schnauzer pups are no exception. When you look at a litter you will be entranced; each pup seems to have its own very individual character. But this is a situation where you must not let your heart rule your head.

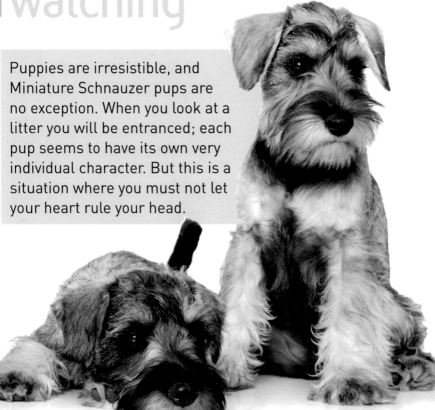

Always remember that you are making a long-term commitment, so you need to be 100 per cent confident that the breeding stock is healthy, and the puppies have been reared with love and care.

Viewing a litter

It is a good idea to have mental checklist of what to look out for when you visit a breeder. You want to see:

- A clean, hygienic environment.

- Puppies that are out-going and friendly, and eager to meet you.

- A sweet-natured mother ready to show off her babies.

- Puppies that are well covered, but not pot-bellied, which could be an indication of worms.

- Coats should look clean and healthy with no sign of scurf or sore patches.

- Bright eyes, with no sign of soreness or discharge.

- Clean ears that smell fresh.

- No discharge from the nose.

- Clean rear ends – matting could indicate upset tummies.

- Lively pups that are keen to play.

It is important that you see the mother with her puppies, as this will give you an idea of the temperament they are likely to inherit. It is also helpful if you can see other close relatives so you can see the type of Mini Schnauzer the breeder produces.

In most cases, you will not be able to see the father (sire) as most breeders will travel some distance to find a stud dog that is not too close to their own bloodlines and complements their bitch. However, you should be able to see photos of him and be given the chance to examine his pedigree and show record.

Companion puppy

If you are looking for a Miniature Schnauzer as a companion, you should be guided by the breeder, who will have spent hours and hours puppy watching, and will know each of the pups as individuals. It is tempting to choose a puppy yourself, but the breeder will take into account your family set up and lifestyle and will help you to pick the most suitable puppy.

Show puppy

If you are buying a puppy with the hope of showing him, make sure you make this clear to the breeder. A lot of planning goes into producing a litter, and

although all the puppies will have been reared with equal care, there will be one or two that have show potential.

Ideally, recruit a breed expert to inspect the puppies with you, so you have the benefit of an objective evaluation. The breeder will also help with your choice as they will want to ensure that only the best of their stock is exhibited in the show ring.

Look out for a puppy with the following attributes:

- A well-balanced, square body, where the length of the body equals the height to the shoulders.

- The depth of the body should equal the length of the leg.

- The head should be brick-shaped.

- The eyes must be dark, and the lips, nose and pads should be black.

- The top jaw should be slightly more forward than the lower jaw so, as the pup develops, he will acquire the correct scissor bite (see page 28), although this cannot be guaranteed to remain correct when the adult teeth come in.

- A tail that is set on high.

- Signs of a harsh coat growing underneath the puppy coat.

- When trotting, a pup should have a clean action in front with the legs moving in a straight line.

- An extrovert, out-going temperament.

It is easier to choose a Miniature Schnauzer puppy than many other breeds because what you see at eight weeks is, generally, what you will see as an adult. However, there are no guarantees, and if your Mini Schnauzer fails to make the grade in the show ring, he will still be an outstanding companion and a much-loved member of your family.

A Miniature Schnauzer-friendly home

It may seem an age before your Miniature Schnauzer puppy is ready to leave the breeder and move to his new home. But you can fill the time by getting your home ready, and buying the equipment you will need. These preparations apply to a new puppy but, in reality, they are the means of creating an environment that is safe and secure for your Mini Schnauzer throughout his life.

In the home

The Miniature Schnauzer is always alert, on the lookout for anything that appears new and interesting. If you add in a puppy's natural curiosity, you will see that your house is one big playground. Of course, you want your puppy to have fun, but the top priority is to keep him safe.

The best plan is to decide which rooms your Mini Schnauzer will have access to, and make these areas puppy friendly. Trailing electric cables are a major hazard and these will need to be out of reach. Make sure all cupboards are secure, particularly in the kitchen where you may store cleaning materials which could be toxic to dogs. Household plants can also be poisonous, so these will need to relocated, along with breakable ornaments.

Your puppy will be too small to negotiate stairs to begin with, so it may be easier to make upstairs off-limits right from the start. The best way of doing this is to use a baby gate, making sure your puppy cannot squeeze through, which could result in injury.

In the garden

The Miniature Schnauzer is not a big dog, but he is surprisingly agile, so you need to check boundary fencing is secure and of a suitable height. In fact, the Mini Schnauzer is not great escape artist; he sees his role as a watchdog, patrolling the boundaries, but it is better to be safe than sorry. Gates leading from the garden should be checked to ensure they have secure fastenings.

If you are a keen gardener, you may want to protect your prized plants from unwanted attention. There are a number of flowers and shrubs that are toxic to dogs, so check this out on the Internet (www.dogbooksonline.co.uk/caring/poisonous-plants/) or by seeking advice from your local garden centre. You will also need to designate a toileting area. This will assist the house training process, and it will also make cleaning up easier. For information on house-training, see page 92.

House rules

Before your puppy comes home, hold a family conference to decide on the house rules. For example, is your Mini Schnauzer going to be allowed to roam downstairs, or will you keep him in the kitchen unless you can supervise him elsewhere? When he is in the sitting room, is he allowed to come on your lap for a cuddle? These are personal choices, but once you have let your puppy to do something, he will think that this is 'allowed', regardless of whether you change your mind. You and your family must make decisions – and stick with them – otherwise your puppy will be upset and confused, not understanding what you want of him.

Buying equipment

There are some essential items of equipment you will need for your Miniature Schanuzer. If you choose wisely, much of it will last for many years to come.

Indoor crate

Rearing a puppy is so much easier if you invest in an indoor crate. It provides a safe haven for your puppy at night, when you have to go out during the day, and at other times when you cannot supervise him. A puppy needs a base where he feels safe and secure, and where he can rest undisturbed. An indoor crate provides the perfect den, and many adults continue to use them throughout their lives. It is therefore important to buy a crate that is large enough for your Mini Schnauzer when he is fully grown.

You will also need to consider where you are going to locate the crate. The kitchen is usually the most suitable place as this is the hub of family life. Try to find a snug corner where the puppy can rest when he wants to, but where he can also see what is going on around him, and still be with the family.

Beds and bedding

The crate will need to be lined with bedding and the best type to buy is synthetic fleece. This is warm and cosy, and as moisture soaks through it, your puppy will not have a wet bed

when he is tiny and is still unable to go through the night without relieving himself. This type of bedding is machine washable and easy to dry; buy two pieces, so you have one to use while the other piece is in the wash.

If you have purchased a crate, you may not feel the need to buy an extra bed, although many Mini Schnauzers like to have a bed in the family room so they feel part of household activities. There is an amazing array of dog-beds to chose from – duvets, bean bags, cushions, baskets, igloos, mini-four posters – so you can take your pick! Before you make a major investment, wait until your puppy has gone through the chewing phase; you will be surprised at how much damage can be inflicted by small teeth.

Collar and leash

You may think that it is not worth buying a collar for the first few weeks, but the sooner your pup gets used to it, the better. All you need is a lightweight baby collar; you can buy something more exotic when your Mini Schnauzer is fully grown.

A nylon leash is suitable for early training, but make sure the fastening is secure. Again, you can invest in a more expensive leash at a later date – there are lots of attractive collar and leash sets to choose from.

ID

Your Miniature Schnauzer needs to wear some form of ID when he is out in public places. This can be in the form of a disc, engraved with your contact details, attached to the collar. When your Mini Schnauzer is full-grown, you can buy an embroidered collar with your contact details, which eliminates the danger of the disc becoming detached from the collar.

You may also wish to consider a permanent form of ID. Increasingly, breeders are getting puppies' micro-chipped before they go to their new homes. A microchip is the size of a grain of rice. It is 'injected' under the skin, usually between the shoulder blades, with a special needle. It has some tiny barbs on it, which dig into the tissue around where it lies, so it does not migrate from that spot.

Each chip has its own unique identification number which can only be read by a special scanner. That ID number is then registered on a national database with your name and details, so that if ever your dog is lost, he can be taken to any vet or rescue centre where he is scanned and then you are contacted.

If your puppy has not been micro-chipped, you can ask your vet to do it, maybe when he goes along for his vaccinations.

Bowls

Your Mini Schnauzer will need two bowls; one for food, and one for fresh drinking water, which should always be readily available. A stainless steel bowl is a good choice for a food bowl as it is tough and hygienic. Plastic bowls may be chewed, and there is a danger that bacteria can collect in the small cracks that may appear.

You can opt for a second stainless steel bowl for drinking water, or you may prefer a heavier ceramic bowl, which will not be knocked over so easily.

Food

The breeder will let you know what your puppy is eating and should provide a full diet sheet to guide you through the first six months of your puppy's feeding regime – how much he is eating per meal, how many meals per day, when to increase the amounts given per meal and when to reduce the meals per day.

The breeder may provide you with some food when you collect your puppy, but it is worth making enquiries in advance about the availability of the brand that is recommended.

Grooming equipment

The Miniature Schnauzer needs extensive coat care throughout his life, and unless you use the services of a professional groomer, it will involve buying a lot of grooming equipment. The best plan is to buy what you require for a puppy, and then invest in more equipment as you need it.

For a puppy you will need the following:

- A small, soft slicker brush
- A small, fine comb
- A large metal comb
- Nail clippers
- Toothbrush and toothpaste.

Toys

The Miniature Schnauzer loves to play, and, as far as he is concerned, this means wreaking havoc with his toys. You will be surprised at how much damage a puppy's milk teeth can inflict, and adults can rip soft toys to shreds in a matter of minutes. You therefore need to provide robust toys, such as tug toys, and hard rubber kongs, which will stand up to a Mini Schnauzer.

You should also get into the habit of checking toys on a regular basis for signs of wear and tear. If your puppy swallows a chunk of rubber or plastic, it could cause an internal blockage. This could involve costly surgery to remove the offending item, or at worst, it could prove fatal.

Finding a vet

Before your puppy arrives home, you should register with a vet. Visit some of the vets in your local area, and speak to other pet owners that you might know, to see who they recommend. It is so important to find a good vet, almost as much as finding a good doctor for yourself. You need to find someone you can build up a good rapport with and have complete faith in. Word of mouth is really the best recommendation.

Facing page: The toys you buy must be suitably robust.

When you contact a veterinary practice, find out the following:

- Does the surgery run an appointment system?

- What are the arrangements for emergency, out of hours cover?

- Do any of the vets in the practice have experience treating Miniature Schnauzers?

- What facilities are available at the practice?

If you are satisfied with what your find, and the staff appear to be helpful and friendly, book an appointment so your puppy can have a health check a couple of days after you collect him.

Settling in

When you first arrive home with your puppy, be careful not to overwhelm him. You and your family are hugely excited, but the puppy is in a completely strange environment with new sounds, smells and sights, which is a daunting experience, even for the boldest of pups.

The majority of Miniature Schnauzer puppies are very confident: exploring their new surroundings, wanting to play straightaway and quickly making friends. Others need a little longer to find their feet. Keep a close check on your puppy's body language and reactions so you can proceed at a pace he is comfortable with.

First, let him explore the garden. He will probably need to relieve himself after the journey home, so take him to the allocated toileting area and when he performs give him plenty of praise.

When you take your puppy indoors, let him investigate again. Show him his crate, and encourage him to go in by throwing in a treat. Let him have a sniff, and allow

him to go in and out as he wants to. Later on, when he is tired, you can put him in the crate while you stay in the room. In this way he will learn to settle and will not think he is being abandoned.

It is a good idea to feed your puppy in his crate, at least to begin with, as this helps to build up a positive association. It will not be long before your Miniature Schnauzer sees his crate as his own special den and will go there as a matter of choice. Some owners place a blanket over the crate, covering the back and sides, so that it is even more cosy and den-like.

Meeting the family

Resist the temptation of inviting friends and neighbors to come and meet the new arrival; your puppy needs to focus on getting to know his new family for the first few days. Try not to swamp your Mini Schnauzer with too much attention; there will be plenty of time for cuddles later on!

If you have children in the family, you need to keep everything as calm as possible. Your puppy may not have met children before, and even if he has, he will still find them strange and unpredictable. A puppy can easily become alarmed by too much noise, or he may go to the opposite extreme and become over-excited, which can lead to mouthing and nipping.

The best plan is to get the children to sit on the floor and give them all a treat. Each child can then call the puppy, stroke him, and offer a treat. In this way the puppy is making the decisions rather than being forced into interactions he may find stressful.

If he tries to nip or mouth, make sure there is a toy at the ready, so his attention can be diverted to something he is allowed to bite. If you do this consistently, he will learn to inhibit his desire to mouth when he is interacting with people.

Right from the start, impose a rule that the children are not allowed to pick up or carry the puppy. They can cuddle him when they are sitting on the floor. This may sound a little severe, but a wriggly puppy can be dropped in an instant, sometimes with disastrous consequences

Involve all family members with the day-to-day care of your puppy; this will enable the bond to develop with the whole family as opposed to just one person. Encourage the children to train and reward the puppy, teaching him to follow their commands without question.

The animal family

Miniature Schnauzers are sociable and enjoy the company of other dogs, but if you already own a dog, make sure you supervise early interactions so relations get off on a good footing.

Your adult dog may be allowed to meet the puppy at the breeder's home, which is ideal as the older dog will not feel threatened if he is away from his own home. But if this is not possible, allow your dog to smell the puppy's bedding (the bedding supplied by the breeder is fine) before they actually meet so he familiarizes himself with the puppy's scent.

The garden is the best place for introducing the puppy, as the adult will regard it as neutral territory. He will probably take a great interest in the puppy and sniff him all over. Most puppies are naturally submissive in this situation, and your pup may lick the other dog's mouth or roll over on to his back. Try not to interfere as this is the natural way that dogs get to know each other.

You will only need to intervene if the older dog is too boisterous, and alarms the puppy. In this case, it is a good idea to put the adult on his lead so you have some measure of control.

It rarely takes long for an adult to accept a puppy, particularly if you make a big fuss of the older dog so that he still feels special. However, do not take any risks and supervise all interactions for the first few weeks. If you do need to leave the dogs alone, always make sure your puppy is safe in his crate.

Meeting a cat should be supervised in a similar way, but do not allow your puppy to be rough as the cat may retaliate using its sharp claws. A Miniature Schnauzer puppy is likely to be highly excited by the sight of a new furry friend, and will probably run up and bark in the cat's face. Make sure you stop this straightaway before bad habits develop. The best way to do this is to keep distracting your puppy by calling him to you and offering him treats. In this way, he will switch his focus from the cat to you, and you can reward him for his 'good' behavior.

Generally, the canine-feline relationship should not cause any serious problems. Indeed, many Mini Schnauzers count the family cat among their best friends!

Feeding

The breeder will generally provide enough food for the first few days so the puppy does not have to cope with a change in diet – and possible digestive upset – along with all the stress of moving home.

Some puppies eat up their food from the first meal onwards, others are more concerned by their new surroundings and are too distracted to eat. Do not worry unduly if your puppy seems disinterested in his food for the first day or so. Give him 10 minutes to eat what he wants and then remove the leftovers and start afresh at the next meal.

Do not make the mistake of trying to tempt his appetite with tasty treats or you will end up with a faddy feeder. This is a mistake that is easily made, and a scenario can develop where the dog holds out, refusing to eat his food, in the hope that something better will be offered.

Obviously if you have any concerns about your puppy in the first few days, seek advice from your vet.

The first night

Your puppy will have spent the first weeks of his life either with his mother or curled up with his siblings. He is then taken from everything he knows as familiar, lavished with attention by his new family – and then comes bed time when he is left all alone. It is little wonder that he feels abandoned.

The best plan is to establish a night-time routine, and then stick to it so that your puppy knows what is expected of him. Take your puppy out into the garden to relieve himself, and then settle him in his crate. Some people leave a low light on for the puppy at night for the first week, others have tried a radio as company or a ticking clock. A covered hot-water bottle, filled with warm water, can also be a comfort. Like people, puppies are all individuals and what works for one, does not necessarily work for another, so it is a matter of trial and error.

Be very positive when you leave your puppy on his own; do not linger, or keep returning – this will make the situation more difficult. It is inevitable that he will protest to begin with, but stick to your routine he will soon accept that he gets left at night, but you always return in the morning.

Rescued dogs

Settling an older, rescued dog in the home is very similar to a puppy in as much as you will need to make the same preparations regarding his homecoming. As with a puppy, an older dog will need you to be consistent, so start as you mean to go on.

There is often an initial honeymoon period when you bring a rescued dog home, where he will be on his best behavior for the first few weeks. It is after this period that the true nature of the dog will show, so be prepared for subtle changes in his behavior. It may be advisable to register with a reputable training club, so you can seek advice on any training or behavioral issues at an early stage.

Above all, remember that a rescued dog ceases to be a rescued dog the moment he enters his forever home and should be treated normally, like any other family dog.

A rescued dog may need time to settle into his new home.

House
training

This is an aspect of training that most first-time puppy owners dread, but it should not be a problem as long as you are prepared to put in the time and effort.

Some breeders start the house training process by providing the litter with paper or training pads so they learn to keep their sleeping quarters clean. This is a step in the right direction, but most pet owners want their puppies to toilet outside.

As discussed earlier, you will have allocated a toileting area in your garden when preparing for your puppy's homecoming. You need to take your puppy to this area every time he needs to relieve himself so he builds up an association and knows why you have brought him out to the garden.

Establish a routine and make sure you take your puppy out at the following times:

- First thing in the morning
- After mealtimes
- On waking from a sleep
- Following a play session
- Last thing at night.

A puppy should be taken out to relieve himself every two hours as an absolute minimum. If you can manage an hourly trip, so much the better. The more often your puppy gets it right, the quicker he will learn to be clean in the house. It helps if you use a verbal cue, such as "Busy", when your pup is performing and, in time, this will trigger the desired response.

Do not be tempted to put your puppy out on the doorstep in the hope that he will toilet on his own. Most pups simply sit there, waiting to get back inside the house! No matter how bad the weather is, accompany your puppy and give him lots of praise when he performs correctly.

Vigilance is the key to successful house training.

Do not rush back inside as soon as he has finished, your puppy might start to delay in the hope of prolonging his time outside with you. Praise him, have a quick game – and then you can both return indoors.

When accidents happen

No matter how vigilant you are, there are bound to be accidents. If you witness the accident, take your puppy outside immediately, and give him lots of praise if he finishes his business out there.

If you are not there when he has an accident, do not scold him when you discover what has happened. He will not remember what he has done and will not understand why you are cross with him. Simply clean it up and resolve to be more vigilant next time.

Make sure use a deodorizer, available in pet stores, when you clean up, otherwise your pup will be drawn to the smell and may be tempted to use the same spot again.

Facing page:
Remember, lapses
in house training are
usually your fault!

Choosing
a diet

There are so many different types of
dog food on sale – all claiming to be
the best – so how do you know what is
likely to suit your Miniature Schnauzer?
This is an active breed that needs
a well-balanced diet suited to his
individual requirements.

When choosing a diet, there are basically three
categories to choose from:

Complete

This is probably the most popular diet as it is easy
to feed and is specially formulated with all the
nutrients your dog needs. This means that you
should not add any supplements or you may upset
the nutritional balance.

Most complete diets come in different life stages
– puppy, adult maintenance and senior – so this

means that your Miniature Schnauzer is getting what he needs when he is growing, during adulthood, and as he ages. You can even get prescription diets for dogs with particular health issues.

There are many different brands to choose from so it is advisable to seek advice from your puppy's breeder who will have lengthy experience of feeding Mini Schnauzers.

Canned/pouches

This type of food is usually fed with hard biscuit, and most Miniature Schnauzers find it very appetizing. However, the ingredients – and the nutritional value – do vary significantly between the different brands so you will need to check the label. This type of food often has a high moisture content, so you need to be sure your Mini Schnauzer is getting all the nutrition he needs.

Homemade

There are some owners who like to prepare meals especially for their dogs – and it is probably much appreciated. The danger is that although the food is tasty, and your Miniature Schnauzer may appreciate the variety, you cannot be sure that it has the correct nutritional balance.

If this is a route you want to go down, you will need

A growing puppy needs a high-quality, well-balanced diet.

to find out the exact ratio of fats, carbohydrates, proteins, minerals and vitamins that are needed, which is quite an undertaking.

The Barf (Biologically Appropriate Raw Food) diet is another, more natural approach to feeding. Dogs are fed a diet mimicking what they would have eaten in the wild, consisting of raw meat, bone, muscle, fat, and vegetable matter. This can be labour intensive if you buy all the ingredients yourself, but there are now pre-packed versions, which are available from specialist stockists.

Feeding regime

When your puppy arrives in his new home he will need four meals, evenly spaced throughout the day. You may decide to keep to the diet recommended by your puppy's breeder, and if your pup is thriving there is no need to change. However, if your puppy is not doing well on the food, or you have problems with supply, you will need to make a switch.

When changing diets, it is very important to do it gradually, swapping over from one food to the next, a little at a time, and spreading the transition over a week to 10 days. This will avoid the risk of digestive upset.

When your puppy is around 12 weeks, you can cut out one of his meals; he may well have started to leave some of his food indicating he is ready to do this. By six months, he can move on to two meals a day – a regime that will suit him for the rest of his life.

Bones and chews should be provided under supervision.

Bones and chews

Puppies love to chew, and many adults also enjoy gnawing on a bone. Bones should always be hard and uncooked; rib bones and poultry bones must be avoided as they can splinter and cause major problems. Dental chews, and many of the manufactured rawhide chews are safe, but they should only be given under supervision.

Ideal weight

In order to keep your Miniature Schnauzer in good health it is necessary to monitor his weight. It is all too easy for the pounds to pile on, and this can result in serious health problems.

The Mini Schnauzer takes food very seriously and has perfected the art of fixing you with a gaze and telling you he is 'starving'. You will therefore need to harden your heart and think of your dog's figure! If you are using treats for training, remember to take these into calculation and reduce the amount you feed at his next meal.

When you are assessing your dog's weight, look at him from above, and make sure you can see a definite 'waist'. You should be able to feel his ribs, but not see them.

In order to keep a close check on your Mini Schnauzer's weight, get into the habit of visiting your veterinary surgery on a monthly basis so that you can weigh him. You can keep a record of his weight so you can make adjustments if necessary.

If you are concerned that your Miniature Schnauzer is putting on too much weight – or appears to be losing weight – consult your vet who will help you to plan a suitable diet.

Facing page: A lean, fit Mini Schnauzer will live a longer, healthier life.

Caring for your Mini Schnauzer

The Miniature Schnauzer is a dog of contrasts; he is easy to care for in terms of diet and exercise, but he is definitely high maintenance when it comes to coat care.

Puppy grooming

A Miniature Schnauzer will spend a relatively large proportion of his life on the grooming table, so it is important that he learns to enjoy the attention. If a dog dislikes being handled, major problems can develop; so much so that he may even become aggressive when any attempt is made to groom him.

All these problems are easily avoided if your puppy is accustomed to being groomed and handled from an early age. In fact, many dogs positively enjoy

grooming sessions, viewing them as quality time spent with their owner.

The first task is to teach your puppy to stand on a table. It does not have to be a purpose-built grooming table – just one that is steady and is the right height for you to attend to your Mini Schnauzer without getting backache. Place a rubber mat on the table so your puppy does not slip and, to start with, let him sit or stand while you stroke him, and praise him for being calm. Reward him with a treat, and that will be sufficient for the first session.

The next day, you can introduce a slicker bush, and groom him for a few minutes. The breeder will have introduced grooming, so once your puppy feels confident with you, he should start to relax. You will then need to comb through the longer hair (furnishings) on the legs and hindquarters and the beard. A wide-toothed metal comb is best for this job, and then use a small, fine-toothed comb for the eyebrows. When your puppy first arrives home, he will not have much in the way of furnishings, but it is important that he gets used to the procedure.

Adult grooming

The Miniature Schnauzer's adult coat consists of a soft but dense undercoat and a harsh, wiry topcoat. You will find it much easier to allocate a few minutes every day to grooming, rather than allowing the coat to become matted and tangled.

As with a puppy, you will need to work though the body coat with a slicker brush, and then comb through the furnishings, teasing out any knots that appear. As the coat grows, the beard will need special attention as it can become soiled with food and other debris.

The beard and the skirt (the underside) will also need trimming, otherwise they become long and straggly, and impossible to manage. You can learn how to do this yourself, or you can have it done when your dog goes to a professional groomer to be clipped.

Bathing

There is no need to bath your Miniature Schnauzer on a regular basis, as bathing will have an adverse effect on the coat. Most pet owners reserve a full bath for those times when their dog has rolled in something particularly smelly...

However, the beard and the leg furnishing should be washed once a week, using a shampoo and conditioner that is specially formulated for dogs.

Clipping

Most owners of pet Miniature Schnauzers opt to maintain the coat by having it clipped. This looks very smart and certainly cuts down on the huge workload associated with hand stripping and scissoring.

On average, your Miniature Schnauzer will need to be clipped by a professional groomer every six weeks, which involves clipping the top of the head, cheeks, throat, chest, and body.

Show presentation

There is nothing wrong with having your pet Miniature Schnauzer clipped – indeed, it is the best way of caring for his coat. However, it will not do for a show dog. The process of clipping destroys the harsh, wiry texture of the coat, and so show dogs must be hand-stripped.

This is a laborious process which involves pulling out the dead hair with finger and thumb. All areas are stripped, except for the cheeks, throat, ears, underside and rear which are clipped. The legs, eyebrows and beard are scissored.

Most groomers work on the coat continually, gradually enhancing the shape so the dog looks his best in the show ring. There is a huge amount

Accustom your puppy to grooming from an early stage.

The workload increases as the adult coat comes through.

Pet dogs are generally clipped.

of skill involved – as well as a lot of expensive grooming equipment – so it is definitely a job for the professionals.

Routine care

In addition to grooming, you will need to carry out some routine care.

Eyes

Check the eyes for signs of soreness or discharge. You can use cotton (cotton-wool), a separate piece for each eye, and wipe away any debris.

Ears

The ears should be clean and free from odor. You can buy specially manufactured ear wipes, or you can use a piece of cotton to clean them if necessary. Do not probe into the ear canal or you risk doing more harm than good.

You will also need to pluck the hair that grows inside the ear. This is most easily done using finger and thumb, or you can use tweezers. The process is made easier if you use an ear powder; the hair comes out more easily and causes less distress. Start doing this from an early age, rewarding your puppy for his co-operation, so he learns to accept it without a fuss.

Show dogs need to have their coat stripped, using a stripping knife or finger and thumb.

The clippers will be needed on certain parts of the coat, such as the ears.

Scissors are used to enhance the lines and to accentuate the bushy eyebrows.

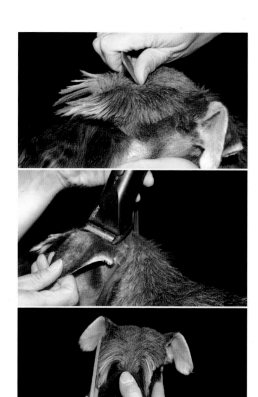

Teeth

Dental disease is becoming more prevalent among dogs so teeth cleaning should be seen as an essential part of your care regime. The build up of tartar on the teeth can result in tooth decay, gum infection and bad breath, and if it is allowed to accumulate, you may have no option but to get the teeth cleaned under anesthetic.

When your Miniature Schnauzer is still a puppy accustom him to teeth cleaning so it becomes a matter of routine. Dog toothpaste comes in a variety of meaty flavours, which your Mini Schnauzer will like, so you can start by putting some toothpaste on your finger and gently rubbing his teeth. You can then progress to using a finger brush or a toothbrush, whichever you find most convenient.

Remember to reward your Miniature Schnauzer when he co-operates and then he will positively look forward to his teeth-cleaning sessions.

Nails

Nail trimming is a task dreaded by many owners – and many dogs – but, again, if you start early on, your Miniature Schnauzer will get used to the procedure.

Dark nails are harder to trim than white nails as you cannot see the quick (the vein that runs through the nail) and it will bleed if it is nicked. The best policy is to trim little and often so the nails don't grow too long, and you do not risk cutting too much and catching the quick.

If you are worried about trimming your Mini Schnauzer's nails, go to your vet so you can see it done properly. If you are still concerned, you can always use the services of a professional groomer.

Keeping a Mini Schnauzer in a show coat demands huge dedication.

Exercise

The Miniature Schnauzer is lively and energetic and will need regular, varied exercise. Going for walks gives a dog the opportunity to use his nose and investigate new sights and smells, so even if he does not walk for miles, he will appreciate going to new places. The Mini Schnauzer has an excellent sense of smell, and an opportunity to explore new places will be viewed as a great treat.

If, for any reason, your time is limited, it is useful if you can teach your Mini Schnauzer to retrieve a toy. He will expend a lot of energy playing this game and he will also enjoy the mental stimulation. If you have more than one dog, they will burn off a lot of energy playing together. If you have a lone dog, why not find a dog-walking friend (as long as their dog is of sound temperament) and you can all enjoy a sociable time together?

The older Mini Schnauzer

We are fortunate the Miniature Schnauzer has a good life expectancy, and you will not notice any significant changes in your dog until he reaches double figures, or maybe even later.

The older Mini Schnauzer will sleep more, and he may be reluctant to go for longer walks. He may

show signs of stiffness when he gets up from his bed, but these generally ease when he starts moving. Some older Miniature Schnauzers may have impaired vision, and some may become a little deaf, but as long as their senses do not deteriorate dramatically, this is something older dogs learn to live with.

If you treat your older Mini Schnauzer with kindness and consideration, he will enjoy his later years and suffer the minimum of discomfort. It is advisable to switch him over to a senior diet, which is more suited to his needs, and you may need to adjust the quantity, as he will not be burning up the calories as he did when he was younger and more energetic. Make sure his sleeping quarters are warm and free from drafts, and if he gets wet, make sure you dry him thoroughly.

Most important of all, be guided by your Miniature Schnauzer. He will have good days when he feels up to going for a walk, and other days when he would prefer to potter in the garden. If you have a younger dog at home, this may well stimulate your Mini Schnauzer to take more of an interest in what is going on, but make sure he is not pestered, as he needs to rest undisturbed when he is tired.

Letting go

Inevitably there comes a time when your Miniature Schnauzer is not enjoying a good quality of life, and you need to make the painful decision to let him go. We would all wish that our dogs died, painlessly, in their sleep but, unfortunately, this is rarely the case.

However, we can allow our dogs to die with dignity, and to suffer as a little as possible, and this should be our way of saying thank you for the wonderful companionship they have given us.

When you feel the time is drawing close, talk to your vet, who will be able to make an objective assessment of your Mini Schnauzer's condition and will help you to make the right decision.

This is the hardest thing you will ever have to do as a dog owner, and it is only natural to grieve for your beloved Mini Schnauzer. But eventually, you will be able to look back on the happy memories of times spent together, and this will bring much comfort. You may, in time, feel that your life is not complete without a Miniature Schnauzer, and you will feel ready to welcome a new puppy into your home.

Social skills

To live in the modern world, without fears and anxieties, a Miniature Schnauzer needs an education in social skills so that he learns to cope calmly and confidently in a wide variety of situations.

Early learning

The breeder will have started a program of socialization by getting the puppies used to all the sights and sounds of a busy household. You need to continue this when your pup arrives in his new home, making sure he is not worried by household equipment, such as the vacuum cleaner or the washing machine, and that he gets used to unexpected noises from the radio and television.

Remember, it is important that you handle your puppy on a regular basis so he will accept grooming and other routine care, and will not be worried if he has to be examined by the vet.

To begin with, your puppy needs to get used to all the members of his new family, but then you should give him the opportunity to meet friends and others who come to the house. Miniature Schnauzers are natural watchdogs, and while a warning bark is acceptable, you do not want your dog to continue barking at visitors.

Right from the start, teach him acceptable greeting behavior in the following way:

- Have some treats at the ready, and once your puppy has said his first 'hello', distract his attention by calling him to you, giving him a treat and praising him.

- Let him return to the visitor, hopefully not barking, and then call him back to you for a treat and praise. In this way, the pup learns that coming to you is more rewarding.

- Now give the visitor a couple of treats so that when your puppy approaches – and is not barking – he can be rewarded.

This training may take a bit of practice, but it is well worth persevering; the alternative is to invest in some earplugs!

It is also very important that your puppy learns to interact with children. If you do not have children, make sure your puppy has the chance to meet and play with other people's children so he learns that humans come in small sizes, too.

The outside world

When your puppy has completed his vaccinations, he is ready to venture into the outside world. Mini Schnauzer puppies take a lively interest in anything new and will relish the opportunity to broaden their horizons. However, there is a lot for a small puppy to take on board, so do not swamp him with too many new experiences when you first set out.

The best plan is to start in a quiet area with light traffic, and only progress to a busier place when your puppy is ready. There is so much to see and hear – people (maybe carrying bags or umbrellas), pushchairs, bicycles, cars, lorries, machinery – so give your puppy a chance to take it all in.

If he does appear worried, do not fall into the trap of sympathizing with him, or worse still, picking him up. This will only teach your pup that he had a good reason to be worried and, with luck, you will 'rescue' him if he feels scared.

Instead, give him a little space so he does not have to confront whatever he is frightened of, and distract him with a few treats. Then encourage him to walk past, using a calm, no-nonsense approach. Your pup will take the lead from you, and will realize there is nothing to fear.

Facing page: The outside world can appear daunting to a young puppy.

Your pup also needs to continue his education in canine manners, stared by his mother and by his littermates, as he needs to be able to greet all dogs calmly, giving the signals that say he is friendly and offers no threat. If you have a friend who has a dog of sound temperament, this is an ideal beginning. As your puppy gets older and more established, you can widen his circle of canine acquaintances.

Training classes

A training class will give your Miniature Schnauzer the opportunity to interact with other dogs, and he will also learn to focus on you in a different, distracting environment.

Before you go along with your puppy, it is worth attending a class as an observer to make sure you are happy with what goes on.

Find out the following:

- How much training experience do the instructors have?

- Are the classes divided into appropriate age categories?

- Do the instructors have experience training Miniature Schnauzers?

- Do they use positive, reward-based training methods?

- Does the club train for the Good Citizen Scheme (see page 154)?

If the class is well run, it is certainly worth attending. Both you and your Mini Schnauzer will learn useful training exercises; it will increase his social skills, and you will have the chance to talk to lots of like-minded dog enthusiasts.

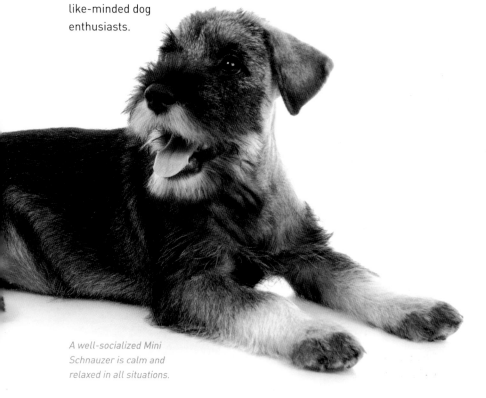

A well-socialized Mini Schnauzer is calm and relaxed in all situations.

Training
guidelines

The Miniature Schnauzer is a highly intelligent dog and he is generally eager to please. However, he is a smart dog with his own ideas, and he will run rings around you unless he learns to respect you and accept your leadership.

You will be keen to get started, but in your rush to get training underway, do not neglect the fundamentals that could make the difference between success and failure.

When you start training, try to observe the following guidelines:

- Choose an area that is free from distractions so your puppy will focus on you. You can move to a more challenging environment as your pup progresses.

- Do not train your puppy just after he has eaten or when you have returned from exercise. He will either be too full, or too tired, to concentrate.

- Do not train if you are in a bad mood, or if you are short of time – these sessions always end in disaster!

- Make sure you have a reward your Mini Schnauzer values – tasty treats, such as cheese or cooked liver, or an extra special toy.

- If you are using treats, make sure they are bite-size, otherwise you will lose momentum when your pup stops to chew on his treat.

- Keep your verbal cues simple, and always use the same one for each exercise. For example, when you ask your puppy to go into the Down position, the cue is "Down", not "Lie Down", Get Down", or anything else... Remember your dog does not speak English; he associates the sound of the word with the action.

- If your Mini Schnauzer is finding an exercise difficult, break it down into small steps so it is easier to understand.

- Do not make your training sessions boring and repetitious; your dog will quickly lose interest.

- Do not train for too long, particularly with a young puppy, which will have a very short attention span, and always end training sessions on a positive note.

- Above all, have fun so you and your Mini Schnauzer both enjoy spending quality time together.

First lessons

A Miniature Schnauzer puppy will soak up new experiences like a sponge, so training should start from the time your pup arrives in his new home. It is so much easier to teach good habits rather than trying to correct your puppy when he has established an undesirable pattern of behavior.

Wearing a collar

Most pet dogs wear a collar on a permanent basis, so it is a good idea to get your pup used to wearing one from an early stage. Even though he may not need to wear a collar in the house, he will on the leash when he goes out in public places, so he needs to get used to the feel of a collar around his neck. The best plan is to accustom your pup to wearing a soft collar for a few minutes at a time until he gets used to it.

You should be able to fit at least two fingers between the collar and his neck. Then have a game to distract

his attention. This will work for a few moments; then he will stop, put his back leg up behind his neck and scratch away at the peculiar itchy thing round his neck, which feels so odd.

Bend down, rotate the collar, pat him on the head and distract him by playing with a toy or giving him a treat. Once he has worn the collar for a few minutes each day, he will soon ignore it and become used to it.

Never leave the collar on the puppy unsupervised, especially when he is outside in the garden, or when he is in his crate, as it is could get snagged, causing serious injury.

Walking on the leash

Once your puppy is used to the collar, take him outside into your secure garden where there are no distractions.

Attach the leash and, to begin with, allow him to wander with the leash trailing, making sure it does not become snagged up. Then pick up the leash and follow the pup wherever he wants to go; he needs to get used to the sensation of being attached to you.

The next stage is to get your Mini Schnauzer to follow you, and for this you will need some tasty treats. You can show him a treat in your hand, and then encourage him to follow you. Walk a few paces,

and if he is co-operating, stop and reward him. If he puts on the brakes, simply change direction and lure him with the treat.

Next, introduce some changes of direction so your puppy is walking confidently alongside you. At this stage, introduce a verbal cue "Heel" when your puppy is in the correct position. You can then graduate to walking your puppy outside the home – as long as he has completed his vaccination program – starting in quiet areas and building up to busier environments.

Do not expect too much of your puppy too soon when you are leash walking away from home. He will be distracted by all the new sights and sounds he encounters, so concentrating on leash training will be difficult for him. Give him a chance to look and see, and reward him frequently when he is walking forward confidently on a loose leash.

Come when called

Teaching a reliable recall is invaluable for both you and your Miniature Schnauzer. You are secure in the knowledge that your dog will come back when he is called, and your Mini Schnauzer benefits from being allowed off the lead and having the freedom to investigate all the exciting new scents he comes across.

The Miniature Schnauzer likes to be with his people, but he also likes to explore his surroundings, and pick up on the local news by using his sense of smell. These are the times when a Mini Schnauzer may become selectively 'deaf' to your calls, and is only ready to 'hear' you when he has finished his investigations. Obviously, you can allow him a little leeway, but you do want a dog that will come when he is called.

The breeder may have started this lesson, simply by calling the puppies to "Come" at mealtimes, or when they are moving from one place to another.

You can build on this when your puppy arrives in his new home, calling him to "Come" when he is in a confined space, such as the kitchen. This is a good place to build up a positive association with the verbal cue – particularly if you ask your puppy to "Come" to get his dinner!

Always reward your Mini Schnauzer when he come back to you.

The next stage is to transfer the lesson to the garden. Arm yourself with some treats, and wait until your puppy is distracted. Then call him, using a higher-pitched, excited tone of voice. At this stage, a puppy wants to be with you, so capitalize on this and keep practicing the verbal cue, and rewarding your puppy with a treat and lots of praise when he comes to you.

Now you are ready to introduce some distractions. Try calling him when someone else is in the garden, or wait a few minutes until he is investigating a really interesting scent. When he responds, make a really big fuss of him and give him some extra treats so he knows it is worth his while to come to you. If your puppy responds, immediately reward him with a treat.

If he is slow to come, run away a few steps and then call again, making yourself sound really exciting. Jump up and down, open your arms wide to welcome him; it doesn't matter how silly you look, he needs to see you as the most fun person in the world.

When you have a reliable recall in the garden, you can venture into the outside world. Do not be too ambitious to begin with; try a recall in a quiet place with the minimum of distractions and only progress to more challenging environments if your Mini Schnauzer is responding well.

Do not make the mistake of only asking your dog to come at the end of a walk. What is the incentive in coming back to you if all you do is clip on his leash and head for home? Instead, call your dog at random times throughout the walk, giving him a treat and a stroke, and then letting him go free again. In this way, coming to you is always rewarding, and does not signal the end of his free run.

Facing page: A reliable recall is key to providing free-running exercise.

Stationary exercises

The Sit and Down are easy to teach, and mastering these exercises will be rewarding for both you and your Miniature Schnauzer.

Sit

The best method is to lure your Mini Schnauzer into position, and for this you can use a treat, a toy, or his food bowl.

- Hold the reward (a treat or food bowl) above his head. As he looks up, he will lower his hindquarters and go into a sit.

- Practice this a few times and when your puppy understands what you are asking, introduce the verbal cue "Sit".

When your Mini Schnauzer understands the exercise, he will respond to the verbal cue alone, and you will not need to reward him every time he sits. However,

Dog Expert

it is a good idea to give him a treat on a random basis when he co-operates to keep him guessing!

Down

This is an important lesson, and can be a lifesaver if an emergency arises and you need to bring your Miniature Schnauzer to an instant halt.

You can start with your dog in a Sit or a Stand for this exercise. Stand or kneel in front of him and show him you have a treat in your hand. Hold the treat just in front of his nose and slowly lower it towards the ground, between his front legs.

As your Mini Schnauzer follows the treat he will go down on his front legs and, in a few moments, his hindquarters will follow. Close your hand over the treat so he doesn't cheat and get the treat before he is in the correct position. As soon as he is in the Down, give him the treat and lots of praise.

Keep practicing, and when your Mini Schnauzer understands what you want, introduce the verbal cue "Down".

Facing page: The Down is one of the most useful exercises you can teach.

Control exercises

These exercises are not the most exciting but they are useful in a variety of different situations. It also teaches your Miniature Schnauzer that you are someone to be respected, and if he co-operates, he is always rewarded for making the right decision.

Wait

This exercise teaches your Mini Schnauzer to "Wait" in position until you give the next command; it differs from the Stay exercise where he must stay where you have left him for a more prolonged period. The most useful application of "Wait" is when you are getting your dog out of the car and you need him to stay in position until you clip on his leash.

Start with your puppy on the leash to give you a greater chance of success. Ask him to "Sit", then stand in front him. Step back one pace, holding your hand, palm flat, facing him. Wait a second and then come back to stand in front of him. You can then reward him and release him with a word, such as "OK".

Practice this a few times, waiting a little longer before you reward him, and then introduce the verbal cue "Wait".

You can reinforce the lesson by using it in different situations, such as asking your Mini Schnauzer to "Wait" before you put his food bowl down.

Stay

You need to differentiate this exercise from the Wait by using a different hand signal and a different verbal cue.

Start with your Miniature Schnauzer in the Down as he most likely to be secure in this position. Stand by his side and then step forward, with your hand held back, palm facing the dog.

Step back, release him, and then reward him. Practice until your Mini Schnauzer understands the exercise and then introduce the verbal cue "Stay".

Gradually increase the distance you can leave your puppy, and increase the challenge by walking around him – and even stepping over him – so that he learns he must "Stay" until you release him.

Leave

A response to this verbal cue means that your Miniature Schnauzer will learn to give up a toy on request, and it follows that he will give up anything when he is asked, which is very useful if he has got hold of a forbidden object. You can also use it if you catch him red-handed raiding the bin, or digging up a prized plant in the garden.

Some Mini Schnauzers can be a little possessive over toys, and some think that running off with a 'trophy' is the greatest fun. This may appear to be harmless, but if your let your Mini Schnauzer get away with it, he will think he has the upper hand and may start to take advantage in other situations. It is therefore important to teach your puppy that if he gives up something, he will get a reward, which may be even better than whatever he had in the first place!

- The "Leave" command can be taught quite easily when you are first playing with your puppy. As you gently take a toy from his mouth, introduce the verbal cue, "Leave", and then praise him.

- If he is reluctant, swap the toy for another toy or a treat. This will usually do the trick.

- Do not try to pull the toy from his mouth if he refuses to give it up, as this will only make him keener to hang on to it. Let the toy go 'dead' in your hand, and then swap it for a new, exciting toy, so this becomes the better option.

- Remember to make a big fuss of your Mini Schnauzer when he co-operates. If he is rewarded with verbal praise, plus a game with a toy or a tasty treat, he will learn that "Leave" is always a good option.

Facing page: If you provide a good 'swap', your Mini Schnauzer will see the point in giving up his toy.

Opportunities for Mini Schnauzers

The Miniature Schnauzer is quick-witted and highly intelligent, and if you have ambitions to try more advanced training or compete in one of the canine disciplines, he will be a willing pupil.

Good Citizen Scheme

The Kennel Club Good Citizen Scheme was introduced to promote responsible dog ownership, and to teach dogs basic good manners. In the US there is one test; in the UK there are four award levels – Puppy Foundation, Bronze, Silver and Gold.

Exercises within the scheme include:

- Walking on leash

- Road walking

- Control at door/gate.

- Food manners

- Recall

- Stay

- Send to bed

- Emergency stop.

Competitive obedience

This is a sport where you are assessed as a dog and handler, completing a series of exercises including heelwork, recalls, retrieves, stays, sendaways and scent discrimination.

The Miniature Schnauzer is more than capable of competing in this discipline, but make sure training is fun, and do not put too much pressure on your dog. The Obedience exercises are relatively simple to begin with, involving heelwork, a recall and stays in the lowest class, and, as your progress through, more exercises are added, and the aids you are allowed to give are reduced.

To achieve top honours in this discipline requires intensive training as precision and accuracy are of paramount importance. However, you must guard against drilling your Mini Schnauzer, as he will quickly lose motivation.

Rally O

If you do not want to get involved in the rigors of Competitive Obedience, you may find that a sport called Rally O is more to your liking.

This is loosely based on obedience, and also has a few exercises borrowed from Agility when you get to the highest levels. Handler and dog must complete a course, in the designated order, which has a variety of different exercises numbering from 12 to 20. The course is timed and the team must complete within the time limit that is set, but there are no bonus marks for speed.

The great advantage of Rally O is that it is very relaxed, and anyone can compete; indeed, it has proved very popular for handlers with disabilities as they are able to work their dogs to a high standard and compete on equal terms with other competitors.

Agility

The Miniature Schnauzer is a natural at this sport, and if you get your dog focused on the equipment, you will be amazed at his speed – and his enthusiasm!

In this sport, the dog completes an obstacle course under the guidance of his owner. You need a good element of control, as the dog completes the course off the leash.

In competition, each dog completes the course individually and is assessed on both time and accuracy. The dog that completes the course with the fewest faults in the fastest time wins the class. The obstacles include an A-frame, a dog-walk, weaving poles, a seesaw, tunnels, and jumps.

Flyball

The Miniature Schnauzer is not a natural retriever, but with training he can enjoy the hurly burly and excitement of competing in Flyball.

This is a team sport where four dogs are selected to run in a relay race against an opposing team. The dogs are sent out by their handlers to jump four hurdles, catch the ball from the flyball box and then return over the hurdles. The teams compete against the clock, and a heat is decided when the fourth dog crosses the finishing line.

Showing

If you plan to exhibit your Miniature Schnauzer in the show ring, you will need to be a dedicated groomer – or employ the services of a professional – to ensure that your dog looks his best when he is inspected by the judge.

You will also need to spend time training your Mini Schnauzer to perform in the show ring. A dog that does not like being handled by the judge, or one that does not walk smartly on the leash, is never going to win top honours, even if he is a top-quality animal. To do well in the ring, a Miniature Schnauzer must have that quality that says: "look at me!", which proves that he is a real showman.

In order to prepare your Mini Schnauzer for the busy show atmosphere, you need to work on his socialisation, and then take him to ringcraft classes so you both learn what is required in the ring.

Showing at the top level is highly addictive, so watch out – once you start, you will never have a free date in your diary!

Heelwork to music

Also known as Canine Freestyle, this activity is becoming increasingly popular. Dog and handler perform a choreographed routine to music, allowing the dog to show off an array of tricks and moves, which delight the crowd. This discipline demands a huge amount of training, but Miniature Schnauzers enjoy the variety that is involved, and there are some who cannot resist the opportunity to show off!

IHealth care

We are fortunate that the Miniature Schnauzer is a healthy dog and, with good routine care, a well-balanced diet, and sufficient exercise, most will experience few health problems.

However, it is your responsibility to put a program of preventative health care in place – and this should start from the moment your puppy, or older dog, arrives in his new home.

Vaccinations

Dogs are subject to a number of contagious diseases. In the old days, these were killers, and resulted in heartbreak for many owners. Vaccinations have been developed, and the occurrence of the major infectious diseases is now very rare. However, this will only remain the case if all pet owners follow a strict policy of vaccinating their dogs.

There are vaccinations available for the following diseases:

Adenovirus: (Canine Adenovirus): This affects the liver; affected dogs have a classic 'blue eye'.

Distemper: A viral disease, which causes chest and gastro-intestinal damage. The brain may also be affected, leading to fits and paralysis.

Parvovirus: Causes severe gastro enteritis, and most commonly affects puppies.

Leptospirosis: This bacterial disease is carried by rats and affects many mammals, including humans. It causes liver and kidney damage.

Rabies: A virus that affects the nervous system and is invariably fatal. The first signs are abnormal behavior, when the infected dog may bite another animal or a person. Paralysis and death follow. Vaccination is compulsory in most countries. In the UK, dogs traveling overseas must be vaccinated.

Kennel Cough: There are several strains of kennel cough, but they all result in a harsh, dry, cough. This disease is rarely fatal; in fact most dogs make a good recovery within a matter of weeks and show few signs of ill health while they are affected. However, kennel cough is highly infectious among dogs that live together so, for this reason, most boarding kennels will insist that your dog is protected by the vaccine, which is given as nose drops.

Lyme Disease: This is a bacterial disease transmitted by ticks (see page 168). The first signs are limping, but the heart, kidneys and nervous system can also be affected. The ticks that transmit the disease occur in specific regions, such as the north-east states of the USA, some of the southern states, California and the upper Mississippi region. Lyme disease is still rare in the UK so vaccinations are not routinely offered.

Vaccination program

In the USA, the American Animal Hospital Association advises vaccination for core diseases, which they list as: distemper, adenovirus, parvovirus and rabies. The requirement for vaccinating for non-core diseases – leptospriosis, lyme disease and kennel cough – should be assessed depending on a dog's individual risk and his likely exposure to the disease.

In the UK, vaccinations are routinely given for distemper, adenovirus, leptospirosis and parvovirus.

In most cases, a puppy will start his vaccinations at around eight weeks of age, with the second part given a fortnight later. However, this does vary depending on the individual policy of veterinary practices, and the incidence of disease in your area.

You should also talk to your vet about whether to give annual booster vaccinations. This depends on an individual dog's levels of immunity, and how long a particular vaccine remains effective.

Parasites

No matter how well you look after your Miniature Schnauzer, you will have to accept that parasites – internal and external – are ever present, and you need to take preventative action.

Internal parasites: As the name suggests, these parasites live inside your dog. Most will find a home in the digestive tract, but there is also a parasite that lives in the heart. If infestation is unchecked, a dog's health will be severely jeopardized, but routine preventative treatment is simple and effective.

External parasites: These parasites live on your dog's body – in his skin and fur, and sometimes in his ears.

Roundworm

This is found in the small intestine, and signs of infestation will be a poor coat, a pot belly, diarrhoea and lethargy. Pregnant mothers should be treated, but it is almost inevitable that parasites will be passed on to the puppies. For this reason, a breeder will start a worming program, which you will need to continue. Ask your vet for advice on treatment, which will need to continue throughout your dog's life.

Tapeworm

Infection occurs when fleas and lice are ingested; the adult worm takes up residence in the small intestine, releasing mobile segments (which contain eggs) that can be seen in a dog's feces as small rice-like grains. The only other obvious sign of infestation is irritation of the anus. Again, routine preventative treatment is required throughout your Mini Schnauzer's life.

Heartworm

This parasite is transmitted by mosquitoes, and so will only occur where these insects thrive. A warm environment is needed for the parasite to develop, so it is more likely to be present in areas with a warm, humid climate. However, it is found in all parts of the USA, although its prevalence does vary. At present, heartworm is rarely seen in the UK.

Heartworm live in the right side of the heart. Larvae can grow up to 14in (35cm) in length. A dog with heartworm is at severe risk from heart failure, so preventative treatment, as advised by your vet, is essential. Dogs living in the USA should have regular blood tests to check for the presence of infection.

Lungworm

Lungworm, or *Angiostrongylus vasorum*, is a parasite that lives in the heart and major blood vessels supplying the lungs. It can cause many problems, such as breathing difficulties, blood-clotting problems, sickness and diarrhoea, seizures, and can even be fatal. The parasite is carried by slugs and snails, and the dog becomes infected when ingesting these, often accidentally when rummaging through undergrowth.

Lungworm is not common, but it is on the increase and a responsible owner should be aware of it. Fortunately, it is easily preventable and even affected dogs usually make a full recovery if treated early enough. Your vet will be able to advise you on the risks in your area and treatment.

Fleas

A dog may carry dog fleas, cat fleas, and even human fleas. The flea stays on the dog only long enough to have a blood meal and to breed, but its presence will result in itching and scratching. If your dog has an allergy to fleas – which is usually a reaction to the

flea's saliva – he will scratch himself until he is raw.

Spot-on treatment, which should be administered on a routine basis, is easy to use and highly effective on all types of fleas. You can also treat your dog with a spray or with insecticidal shampoo. Bear in mind that the whole environment your dog lives in will need to be sprayed, and all other pets living in your home will also need to be treated.

How to detect fleas

You may suspect your dog has fleas, but how can you be sure? There are two methods to try.

Run a fine comb through your dog's coat, and see if you can detect the presence of fleas on the skin, or clinging to the comb. Alternatively, sit your dog on some white paper and rub his back. This will dislodge feces from the fleas, which will be visible as small brown specks. To double check, shake the specks on to some damp cotton (cotton-wool). Flea feces consists of the dried blood taken from the host, so if the specks turn a lighter shade of red, you know your dog has fleas.

Ticks

These are blood-sucking parasites, most frequently found in rural area where sheep or deer are present.

The main danger is their ability to pass lyme disease to both dogs and humans. lyme disease is prevalent in some areas of the USA (see page 162), although it is still rare in the UK. The treatment you give your dog for fleas generally works for ticks, but you should discuss the best product to use with your vet.

How to remove a tick

If you spot a tick on your dog, do not try to pluck it off as you risk leaving the hard mouth-parts embedded in his skin. The best way to remove a tick is to use a fine pair of tweezers or you can buy a tick remover. Grasp the tick head firmly and then pull the tick straight out from the skin. If you are using a tick remover, check the instructions, as some recommend a circular twist when pulling. When you have removed the tick, clean the area with soap and water.

Ear mites

These parasites live in the outer ear canal. The signs of infestation are a brown, waxy discharge, and your dog will continually shake his head and scratch his ear. If you suspect your Miniature Schnauzer has ear mites, a visit to the vet will be need so that medicated ear drops can be prescribed.

Fur mites

These small, white parasites are often referred to as 'walking dandruff'. They cause a scurfy coat and mild itchiness. However, they are zoonotic – transferable to humans – so prompt treatment with an insecticide prescribed by your vet is essential.

Harvest mites

These are picked up from the undergrowth, and can be seen as a bright orange patch on the webbing between the toes, although this can be found elsewhere on the body, such as on the ears flaps. Treatment is effective with the appropriate insecticide.

Skin mites

There are two types of parasite that burrow into a dog's skin. *Demodex canis* is transferred from a mother to her pups while they are feeding. Treatment is with a topical preparation, and sometimes antibiotics are needed.

The other skin mite is *Sarcoptes scabiei*, which causes intense itching and hair loss. It is highly contagious, so all dogs in a household will need to be treated, which involves repeated bathing with a medicated shampoo.

Common
ailments

As with all living animals, dogs can be affected by a variety of ailments. Most can be treated effectively after consulting your vet, who will prescribe appropriate medication and will advise you on care.

Here are some of the more common problems that could affect your Miniature Schnauzer, with advice on how to deal with them.

Anal glands

These are two small sacs on either side of the anus, which produce a dark-brown secretion that dogs use when they mark their territory. The anal glands should empty every time a dog defecates but if they become blocked or impacted, a dog will experience increasing discomfort. He may nibble at his rear end, or 'scoot' his bottom along the ground to relieve the irritation.

Treatment involves a trip to the vet, who will empty the glands manually. It is important to do this without delay or infection may occur.

Dental problems

Vets report that dental problems are becoming

increasingly common among the dog population, and can cause serious discomfort. However, good dental hygiene will do much to minimize gum infection and tooth decay. If tartar accumulates to the extent that you cannot remove it by brushing, the vet will need to intervene. In a situation such as this, an anesthetic will need to be administered so the tartar can be removed manually.

Diarrhoea

There are many reasons why a dog may have diarrhoea, but most commonly it is the result of scavenging, a sudden change of diet, or an adverse reaction to a particular type of food.

If your dog is suffering from diarrhoea, the first step is to withdraw food for a day. It is important that he does not dehydrate, so make sure that fresh drinking water is available. However, drinking too much can increase the diarrhoea, which may be accompanied with vomiting, so limit how much he drinks at any one time.

After allowing the stomach to rest, feed a bland diet, such as white fish or chicken with boiled rice, for a few days. In most cases, your dog's motions will return to normal and you can resume normal feeding, although this should be done gradually.

However, if this fails to work and the diarrhoea persists for more than a few days, you should consult you vet. Your dog may have an infection which needs to be treated with antibiotics, or the diarrhoea may indicate some other problem which needs expert diagnosis.

Ear infections

The Miniature Schnauzer has neat V-shaped ears that drop forwards to the temple. This allows air to circulate and so Schnauzers are not so prone to ear infections as breeds with drop ears. In the case of cropped ears, there is no impediment to air circulation.

A healthy ear is clean with no sign of redness or inflammation, and no evidence of a waxy-brown discharge or a foul odor. If you see your dog scratching his ear, shaking his head, or holding one ear at an odd angle, you will need to consult your vet.

The most likely causes are ear mites, an infection, or there may a foreign body, such as a grass seed, trapped in the ear.

Depending on the cause, treatment is with medicated ear drops, possibly containing antibiotics. If a foreign body is suspected, the vet will need to carry our further investigations.

Eye problems

The Miniature Schnauzer has medium-sized eyes that are set forward. They do not protrude, which is important as breeds with prominent eyes, such as the Pekingese, are vulnerable to injury.

If your Schnauzer's eyes look red and sore, he may be suffering from conjunctivitis. This may, or may not be accompanied with a watery or a crusty discharge. Conjunctivitis can be caused by a bacterial or viral infection, it could be the result of an injury, or it could be an adverse reaction to pollen.

You will need to consult your vet for a correct diagnosis, but in the case of an infection, treatment with medicated eye drops is effective. Conjunctivitis may also be the first sign of more serious inherited eye problems (see page 184).

In some instances, a dog may suffer from dry, itchy eye, which he may further injure through scratching. This condition, known as *keratoconjunctivitis sicca*, may be inherited.

Foreign bodies

In the home, puppies – and some older dogs – cannot resist chewing anything that looks interesting. The toys you choose for your dog should be suitably robust to withstand damage, but children's toys can be irresistible. Some dogs will chew – and swallow – anything from socks, tights, and any other items from the laundry basket to golf balls and stones from the garden. Obviously, these items are indigestible and could cause an obstruction in your dog's intestine, which is potentially lethal.

The signs to look for are vomiting, and a tucked up posture. The dog will often be restless and will look as though he is in pain.

In this situation, you must get your dog to the vet without delay as surgery will be needed to remove the obstruction.

Heatstroke

The Miniature Schnauzer's head structure is without exaggeration, which means that he has a straightforward respiratory system, and does not suffer breathing problems experienced by flat-nosed breeds, such as the Pug or the French Bulldog.

However, all dogs can overheat on hot days, and this can have disastrous consequences. If the weather is warm make sure your Schnauzer always has access to shady areas, and wait for a cooler part of the day before going for a walk. Be extra careful if you leave your Schnauzer in the car, as the temperature can rise dramatically - even on a cloudy day. Heatstroke can happen very rapidly, and unless you are able lower your dog's temperature, it can be fatal.

If your Schnauzer appears to be suffering from heatstroke, lie him flat and work at lowering his temperature by spraying him with cool water and covering him with wet towels. As soon as he has made some recovery, take him to the vet where cold intravenous fluids can be administered.

Lameness/limping

There are a wide variety of reasons why a dog can go lame, from a simple muscle strain, to a fracture, ligament damage, or more complex problems with the joints. If you are concerned about your dog, do not delay in seeking help.

As your Miniature Schnauzer becomes more elderly,

he may suffer from arthritis, which you will see as general stiffness, particularly when he gets up after resting. It will help if you ensure his bed is in a warm draft-free location, and if your Schnauzer gets wet after exercise, you must dry him thoroughly.

If you Schnauzer seems to be in pain, consult your vet who will be able to help with pain relief medication.

For more information on inherited disorders, see page 183.

Skin problems

If your dog is scratching or nibbling at his skin, first check he is free from fleas. There are other external parasites which cause itching and hair loss, but you will need a vet to help you find the culprit.

The Miniature Schnauzer is prone to skin conditions caused by an allergic reaction. This may take the form of intense itching or hot spots. It can be quite an undertaking to find the cause of the allergy, and you will need to follow your vet's advice, which often requires eliminating specific ingredients from the diet, as well as looking at environmental factors.

There is a skin condition, known as Schnauzer Comedo Syndrome, which can be inherited (see page 187).

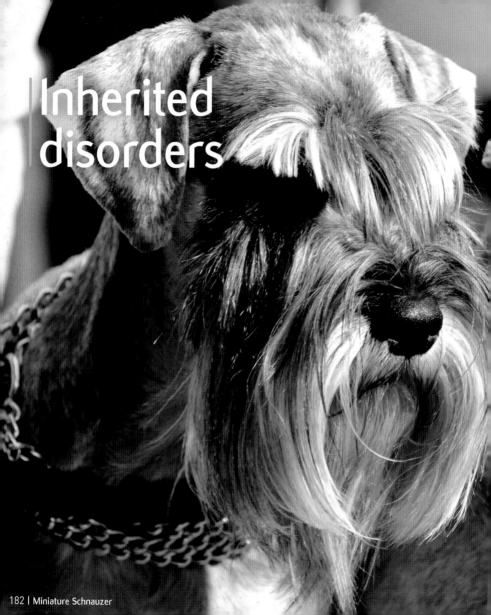

Inherited
disorders

Like all pedigree dogs, the Miniature Schnauzer does have a few breed-related disorders. If diagnosed with any of the diseases listed below, it is important to remember that they can affect offspring so breeding from affected dogs should be discouraged.

There are now recognized screening tests to enable breeders to check for affected individuals and reduce the prevalence of these diseases within the breed.

DNA testing is also becoming more widely available, and as research into the different genetic diseases progresses, more DNA tests are being developed.

Eye disorders

In the US, the Canine Eye Registration Foundation (CERF) was set up by dog-breeders concerned about heritable eye disease, and provides a database of dogs that have been examined by diplomates of the American College of Veterinary Ophthalmologists.

The Miniature Schnauzer may be affected by the following conditions:

Generalised progressive retinal atrophy (GPRA)

This is a bilateral degenerative disease of the cells (rods and cones) of the retina, leading initially to night blindness and progressing to complete loss of vision. Dogs are affected from three to four years of age and there is no cure. There is a test available for younger dogs, before being used for breeding, to prevent carrier individuals passing on the genetic defect.

Hereditary cataracts

Cataracts will affect a dog in a similar way to how humans are affected, by clouding up the lens of the eye and blurring the vision. Two forms of inherited cataract have been recognised in the Miniature Schnauzer. The congenital form is inherited as a recessive trait; puppies can be assessed for it at six to eight weeks old. The developmental form of hereditary cataract occurs in the young or middle-aged dog and can be diagnosed from six months of age.

There are varying degrees of severity; if necessary, surgery is usually successful.

Retinal dysplasia

When the retina develops incorrectly, this may cause impaired vision and blindness depending on the degree of dysplasia and even detachment of the retina from the back of the eye. There are several forms of the disease that Miniature Schnauzers suffer from, varying in severity.

Haemophilia A

Haemophilia is the most common disorder of blood coagulation, inherited in a sex-linked recessive fashion. This means that the male is either affected or clear, whilst females can alternatively be carriers for the trait. Haemophilia A arises from a deficiency of blood clotting Factor VIII.

There are many ways in which Haemophilia A can manifest, at worst as sudden death. There may be early indications, such as prolonged bleeding when the baby teeth are lost or unexpected bruising under the skin. A problem may not become apparent until after surgery such as routine neutering or an injury. Treatment will often require a blood transfusion.

Heart conditions

The Miniature Schnauzer is predisposed to two forms of congenital heart abnormalities.

Patent ductus arteriosus

This involves a connection between the aorta and the pulmonary artery that normally closes at birth or soon after. Surgical intervention will be needed.

Pulmonic stenosis

This condition is present at birth and is caused by an obstruction of blood through the heart's pulmonary valve. Signs are difficulty in breathing and intolerance to exercise, and, in severe cases, will lead to heart failure. Mild cases may not need treatment but medication, and sometimes surgery, will be required in severe cases.

Schnauzer comedo syndrome

This is an inherited skin condition that appears to be confined to Miniature Schnauzers. It is usually spotted after clipping, and involves the formation of comedones along the spinal ridge. These are the result of blocked hair follicles, rather like blackheads in human.

This condition is unsightly rather than serious, and veterinary treatment is only required in the case of bacterial infection. However, dogs suffering from this syndrome cannot be exhibited in the show ring and should not be bred from.

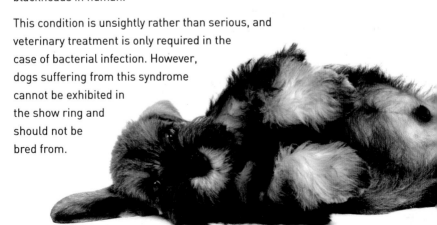

Summing up

It may concern the pet owner to find out about health problems that could affect their dog. But acquiring some basic knowledge is an asset, as it will allow you to spot signs of trouble at an early stage. Early diagnosis is very often the means to the most effective treatment.

Fortunately, the Miniature Schnauzer is a generally healthy and disease-free dog with his only visits to the vet being annual check-ups.

In most cases, owners can look forward to enjoying many happy years with this affectionate and highly entertaining companion.

Useful addresses

Breed & Kennel Clubs
Please contact your Kennel Club to obtain contact information about breed clubs in your area.

UK
The Kennel Club (UK)
1 Clarges Street London, W1J 8AB
Telephone: 0870 606 6750
Fax: 0207 518 1058
Web: www.thekennelclub.org.uk

USA
American Kennel Club (AKC)
5580 Centerview Drive, Raleigh, NC 27606.
Telephone: 919 233 9767
Fax: 919 233 3627
Email: info@akc.org
Web: www.akc.org

United Kennel Club (UKC)
100 E Kilgore Rd, Kalamazoo,
MI 49002-5584, USA.
Tel: 269 343 9020
Fax: 269 343 7037
Web:www.ukcdogs.com

Australia
Australian National Kennel Council (ANKC)
The Australian National Kennel Council is the administrative body for pure breed canine affairs in Australia. It does not, however, deal directly with dog exhibitors, breeders or judges. For information pertaining to breeders, clubs or shows, please contact the relevant State or Territory Body.

International
Fédération Cynologique Internationalé (FCI)
Place Albert 1er, 13, B-6530 Thuin, Belgium.
Tel: +32 71 59.12.38
Fax: +32 71 59.22.29
Web: www.fci.be

Training and behavior
UK
Association of Pet Dog Trainers
Telephone: 01285 810811
Web: www.apdt.co.uk

Canine Behaviour
Association of Pet Behaviour Counsellors
Telephone: 01386 751151
Web: www.apbc.org.uk

USA
Association of Pet Dog Trainers
Tel: 1 800 738 3647
Web: www.apdt.com

American College of Veterinary Behaviorists
Web: dacvb.org

American Veterinary Society of Animal Behavior
Web: www.avsabonline.org

Australia
APDT Australia Inc
Web: www.apdt.com.au

For details of regional behaviorists, contact the relevant State or Territory Controlling Body.

Activities

Agility Club
www.agilityclub.co.uk

British Flyball Association
Telephone: 01628 829623
Web: www.flyball.org.uk

USA
North American Dog Agility Council
Web: www.nadac.com

North American Flyball Association, Inc.
Tel/Fax: 800 318 6312
Web: www.flyball.org

Australia
Agility Dog Association of Australia
Tel: 0423 138 914
Web: www.adaa.com.au

NADAC Australia
Web: www.nadacaustralia.com

Australian Flyball Association
Tel: 0407 337 939
Web: www.flyball.org.au

International
World Canine Freestyle Organisation
Tel: (718) 332-8336
Web: www.worldcaninefreestyle.org

Health

UK
British Small Animal Veterinary Association
Tel: 01452 726700
Web: www.bsava.com

Royal College of Veterinary Surgeons
Tel: 0207 222 2001
Web: www.rcvs.org.uk

www.dogbooksonline.co.uk/healthcare

Alternative Veterinary Medicine Centre
Tel: 01367 710324
Web: www.alternativevet.org

USA
American Veterinary Medical Association
Tel: 800 248 2862
Web: www.avma.org

American College of Veterinary Surgeons
Tel: 301 916 0200
Toll Free: 877 217 2287
Web: www.acvs.org

Canine Eye Registration Foundation
The Veterinary Medical DataBases
1717 Philo Rd, PO Box 3007,
Urbana, IL 61803-3007
Tel: 217-693-4800
Fax: 217-693-4801
Web: www.vmdb.org/cerf.html

Orthopaedic Foundation of Animals
2300 E Nifong Boulevard
Columbia, Missouri, 65201-3806
Tel: 573 442-0418
Fax: 573 875-5073
Web: www.offa.org

American Holistic Veterinary Medical
Association
Tel: 410 569 0795
Web: www.ahvma.org

Australia
Australian Small Animal Veterinary
Association
Tel: 02 9431 5090
Web: www.asava.com.au

Australian Veterinary Association
Tel: 02 9431 5000
Web: www.ava.com.au

Australian College Veterinary Scientists
Tel: 07 3423 2016
Web: acvsc.org.au

Australian Holistic Vets
Web: www.ahv.com.au